SCHOLA

MW01098487

-2

FUN FLAPS
2ND 100 SIGHT WORDS

Violet Findley

New York • Toronto • London
Auckland • Sydney • New Delhi • Hong Kong

Cover and interior design: Michelle H. Kim
Cover photo: Adam Chinitz
Illustrations: The Noun Project

Scholastic Inc., 557 Broadway, New York, NY 10012
ISBN: 978-1-338-60314-9
Copyright © 2020 by Scholastic Inc.
Published by Scholastic Inc. All rights reserved.
Printed in the U.S.A.
First printing, January 2020.

1 2 3 4 5 6 7 8 9 10   40   25 24 23 22 21 20

Table of Contents

INTRODUCTION

Dear Educator,

Welcome to *Fun Flaps: 2nd 100 Sight Words!* These hands-on manipulatives will make learning the second 100 sight words from the Fry List easy and irresistible.

What are sight words? Sight words are those bland connective words—*know, only, very, after, us, should*—that are essential to text, but often a challenge to define and decode. In fact, research shows that as much as 70 percent of everything we read is comprised of them. Predictably, research also shows that children with the ability to automatically recognize sight words are on course to become confident, successful readers. But how do busy teachers and their students find the time?

Enter Fun Flaps! These playful, kinesthetic learning tools will help kids master this important list of words once and for all. Fun Flaps are a great way to foster classroom friendships and enrich family time—just reproduce, fold, and they're ready to use with partners or caregivers. Also, because children are challenged to read sentences aloud, they boost oral language facility. And here's more good news: The book is stocked with companion practice pages to provide children with lots of experience writing these must-know words, too.

So what are you waiting for? Put Fun Flaps into the hands of your students, and watch their literacy skills soar!

Happy Learning,

Violet Findley

P.S. If you like this book, be sure to check out *Fun Flaps: 1st 100 Sight Words*, which, as the title suggests, teaches the first 100 words from the Fry List.

MAKING FUN FLAPS

Making Fun Flaps is so easy. Just reproduce a copy for each child then follow these simple directions.

1 Cut out the Fun Flap along the dashed lines, so you have a square shape.

2 OPTIONAL: Invite children to color the square shape—and pictures—to make the Fun Flap extra engaging.

3 Place the Fun Flap on a flat surface with the blank side facing up.

4 Fold back the four corners along the solid lines so they touch in the center of the square.

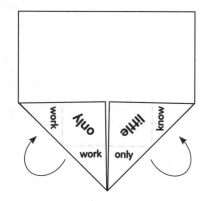

5 Turn over the Fun Flap. Fold back the corners again so that they touch the center of the square.

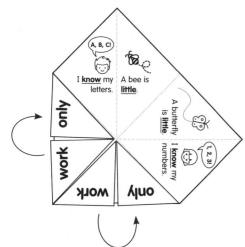

6 Fold the Fun Flap in half.

7 Place your right thumb and index finger inside the two right flaps.

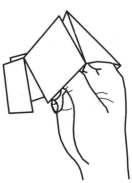

8 Place your left thumb and index finger inside the two left flaps.

9 Open and close the Fun Flap by moving your fingers.

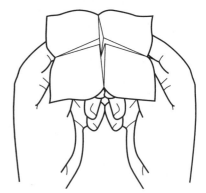

10 Have fun!

TIP

We've included a blank template (and companion writing page), so you—and your students—can create original Fun Flaps to practice additional sight words.

USING FUN FLAPS

Using Fun Flaps is so entertaining. Just follow these simple directions.

1. Partner A holds the fun flap in a closed position, so that the points touch. Partner A asks partner B to choose one of the four featured sight words and a number from 1–10.

2. Partner B chooses a sight word (*know*) and a number (6).

3. Partner A opens and closes the fun flap that many times, inviting Partner B to find the same sight word on the four interior flaps.

4. Partner B points to the sight word (*know*) and reads it aloud.

5. Partner A lifts the flap to reveal a corresponding picture and sight-word sentence (I *know* my letters.), inviting partner B to read it.

6. Partner B reads the sight-word sentence aloud. Tip: Partner A can provide help if necessary.

7. Partners A and B switch roles.

8. Reinforce sight-word learning by encouraging children to use the companion pages to practice writing the featured sight words.

FIVE GREAT WAYS TO USE THE FUN FLAPS

1 Assign partners five minutes of "Fun Flap playtime" at the beginning and/or end of each school day.

2 Place Fun Flaps in a center for kids to enjoy at designated times.

3 Invite classroom volunteers to share Fun Flaps with struggling readers.

4 Send Fun Flaps home so kids can practice their sight words with caregivers.

5 Host a "Fun Flap party," in which kids circulate around the room and use the manipulatives with several different classmates.

TIP

Use Fun Flaps as a way to get students acquainted with one another. Draw names from a hat to pick random partners and foster new friendships!

For a quick and easy assessment technique, type or write the 100 sight words from the fun flaps on separate cards. Next copy the Sight Word Assessment sheets on pages 62 and 63. These sheets allow for individual assessment. Shuffle the sight word cards and hold them up at random for the child to read. If the child reads the word correctly make a ✔ on the sheet. If the child reads the card incorrectly, make an **X**. Then use the fun flaps to reteach the words as needed.

SIGHT WORD ASSESSMENT PART 1

Student's Name: _____

SIGHT WORD	DATE/ ✔ or X	DATE/ ✔ or X	DATE/ ✔ or X	SIGHT WORD	DATE/ ✔ or X	DATE/
over				say		
new				great		
sound				where		
take				help		
only				through		
little				much		
work				before		
know				line		
place				right		
years				too		
live				means		
me				old		
back				any		
give				same		
most				tell		
very				boy		
after				following		
thing				came		
our				want		
just				show		
name				also		
good				around		
sentence				farm		
man				three		
think				small		

62

SIGHT WORD ASSESSMENT PART 2

Student's Name: _____

SIGHT WORD	DATE/ ✔ or X	DATE/ ✔ or X	SIGHT WORD	DATE/ ✔ or X	DATE/ ✔ or X
set			try		
put			kind		
end			hand		
does			picture		
another			again		
well			change		
large			off		
must			play		
big			spell		
even			air		
such			away		
because			animals		
turn			house		
here			point		
why			page		
asked			letters		
went			mother		
men			answer		
read			found		
need			study		
land			still		
different			learn		
home			should		
us			America		
move			world		

63

Connection to the Standards

Using Fun Flaps supports the standards for Reading Foundational Skills for students in grades K–2.

Foundational Skills
Read common high-frequency words by sight.

Print Concepts
Demonstrate understanding of the organization of the basic features of print.

Phonological Awareness
Demonstrate understanding of spoken words, syllables, and sounds.

Fluency
Read with sufficient accuracy and fluency to support comprehension.

Speaking and Listening
Participate in collaborative conversations about age-appropriate topics.

2ND 100 SIGHT WORDS
(From the Fry List)

over	name	boy	such	change
new	good	following	because	off
sound	sentence	came	turn	play
take	man	want	here	spell
only	think	show	why	air
little	say	also	asked	away
work	great	around	went	animals
know	where	farm	men	house
place	help	three	read	point
years	through	small	need	page
live	much	set	land	letters
me	before	put	different	mother
back	line	end	home	answer
give	right	does	us	found
most	too	another	move	study
very	means	well	try	still
after	old	large	kind	learn
thing	any	must	hand	should
our	same	big	picture	America
just	tell	even	again	world

FEATURED SIGHT WORDS

over new sound take

Cut and fold the fun flap.

Name: _____

Trace then practice writing each word.

over over over

new new new new

sound sound sound

take take take take

FEATURED SIGHT WORDS

only little work know

Cut and fold the fun flap.

work

little

know

know

little

only

only

know

work

A butterfly is **little**.

I **know** my numbers.

A bee is **little**.

There is **only** one earth.

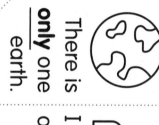

I **know** my letters.

I **work** as a doctor.

There is **only** one sun.

I **work** as a firefighter.

know

little

only

work

only

Name: _____

Trace then practice writing each word.

only only only only

little little little little

work work work

know know know

• © Scholastic Inc.

FEATURED SIGHT WORDS

place years live me

Cut and fold the fun flap.

live

years

me

me

years

place

I am ten **years** old.

This ice cream is for **me**!

I am five **years** old.

This **place** is hard.

This pizza is for **me**!

I **live** in a lake.

me

This **place** is soft.

I **live** in a cave.

live

years

place

live

place

Name: _____

Trace then practice writing each word.

place place place

years years years

live live live live

me me me me me

FEATURED SIGHT WORDS

back give most very

Cut and fold the fun flap.

most

give

very

very

give

I **give** this frog to you.

A turtle is **very** short.

back

I **give** this gift to you.

He went **back** home.

A giraffe is **very** tall.

Most of these toys are balls.

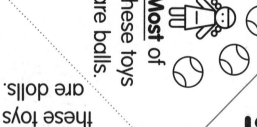

very

She went **back** to school.

Most of these toys are dolls.

most

give

back

most

back

Name: _____

Trace then practice writing each word.

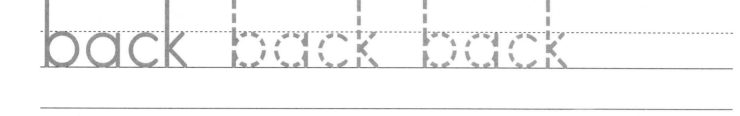

back   back   back

give   give   give   give

most   most   most

very   very   very

© Scholastic Inc.

FEATURED SIGHT WORDS

after thing our just

Cut and fold the fun flap.

our

thing

just

just

thing

after

This **thing** does NOT smell nice.

I **just** love bananas!

This **thing** smells nice.

After day is night.

This is **our** mom.

I **just** love apples!

After night is day.

This is **our** dad.

just

our

thing

after

our

after

Name: _____

Trace then practice writing each word.

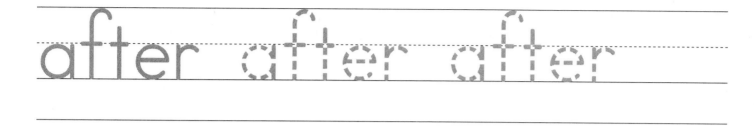

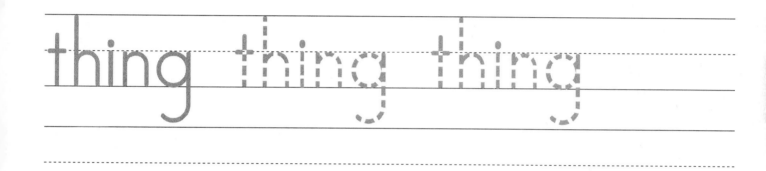

FEATURED SIGHT WORDS

name good sentence man

Cut and fold the fun flap.

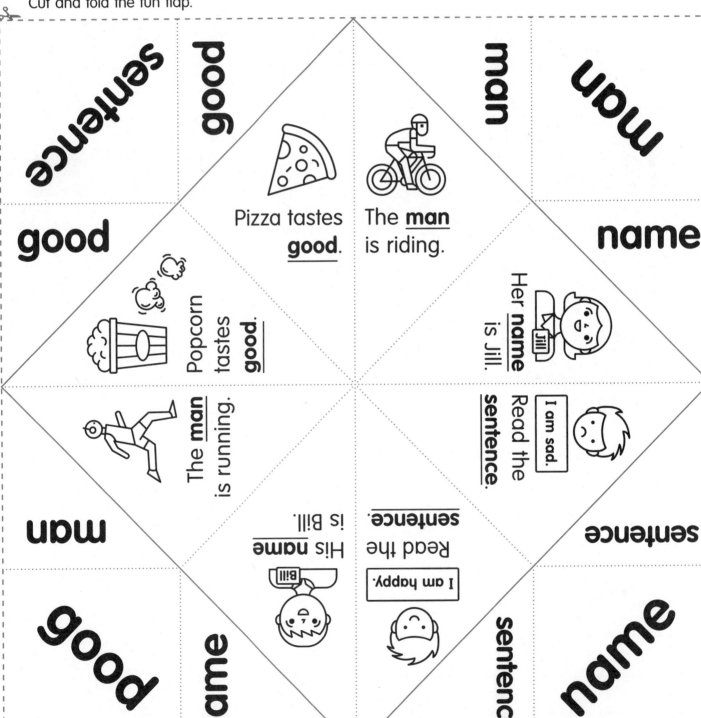

Pizza tastes **good**.

The **man** is riding.

Popcorn tastes **good**.

Her **name** is Jill.

The **man** is running.

Read the **sentence**.

I am sad.

His **name** is Bill.

Read the **sentence**.

I am happy.

sentence

good

good

man

man

name

man

name

sentence

good

name

sentence

name

Name: _____

Trace then practice writing each word.

name name name

good good good

sentence sentence

man man man man

FEATURED SIGHT WORDS

think say great where

Cut and fold the fun flap.

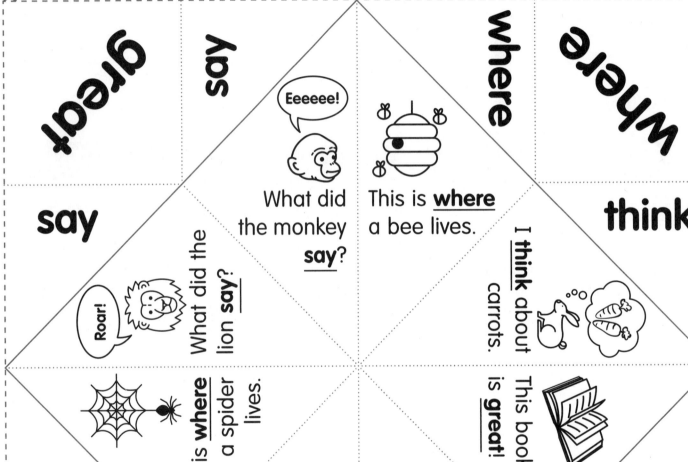

great

say

say

where

say

think

where

think

great

think

great

What did the monkey **say**?

Eeeeee!

This is **where** a bee lives.

What did the lion **say**?

Roar!

I **think** about carrots.

This is **where** a spider lives.

This book is **great**!

This cupcake is **great**!

I **think** about worms.

Name: _____

Trace then practice writing each word.

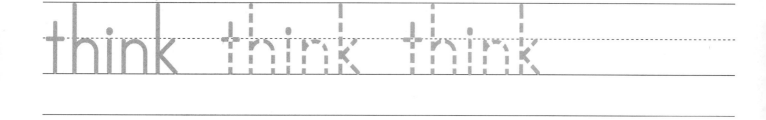

think think think

say say say say

great great great

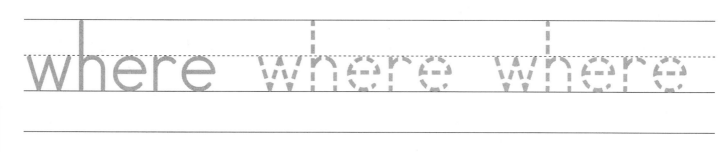

where where where

FEATURED SIGHT WORDS

help through much before

Cut and fold the fun flap.

much

through

before

before

through

help

He looks **through** the window.

I eat **before** I read.

She walks **through** the door.

I **help** clean.

I read **before** I sleep.

There is too **much** trash.

I **help** cook.

There is too **much** rain.

before

much

through

help

much

help

Name: _____

Trace then practice writing each word.

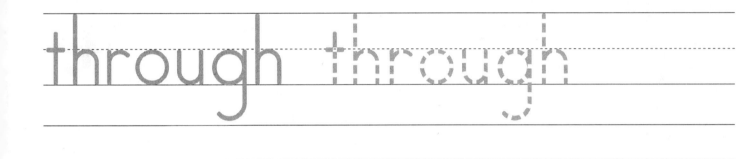

help help help help

through through

much much much

before before

FEATURED SIGHT WORDS

line right too means

Cut and fold the fun flap.

too

right

means

means

right

line

The sad face is on the **right**.

Adios! = Bye!

ADIOS **means** BYE!

The silly face is on the **right**.

I drew a **line**.

There are **too** many bugs!

Hola! = Hello!

HOLA **means** HELLO!

I drew a **line** and a square.

There are **too** many mice!

means

too

right

line

too

line

Name: _____

Trace then practice writing each word.

line line line line

right right right

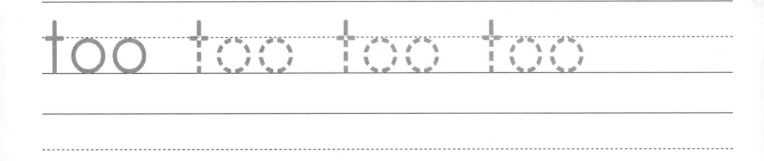

too too too too

means means

FEATURED SIGHT WORDS

old   any   same   tell

Cut and fold the fun flap.

same

any

tell

tell

any

old

There are not **any** candies.

I can **tell** he is sad.

tell

old

There are not **any** cookies.

The chair is **old**.

I can **tell** he is happy.

The cats are the **same**.

same

The hat is **old**.

The dogs are the **same**.

any

old

same

old

28 • © Scholastic Inc.

Name: _____

Trace then practice writing each word.

old   old   old   old   old

any   any   any   any

same   same   same

tell   tell   tell   tell   tell

FEATURED SIGHT WORDS

boy following came want

Cut and fold the fun flap.

came

following

want

want

following

boy

A cat is **following** her.

I **want** that ball!

A dog is **following** her.

A **boy** is jumping.

I **want** that book!

A monster **came**!

A **boy** is swimming.

A clown **came**!

want

came

want

following

boy

came

boy

following

Name: _____

Trace then practice writing each word.

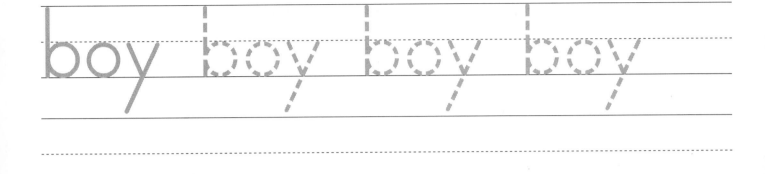

boy boy boy boy

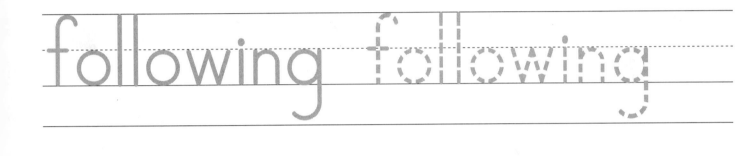

following following

came came came

want want want

FEATURED SIGHT WORDS

show also around farm

Cut and fold the fun flap.

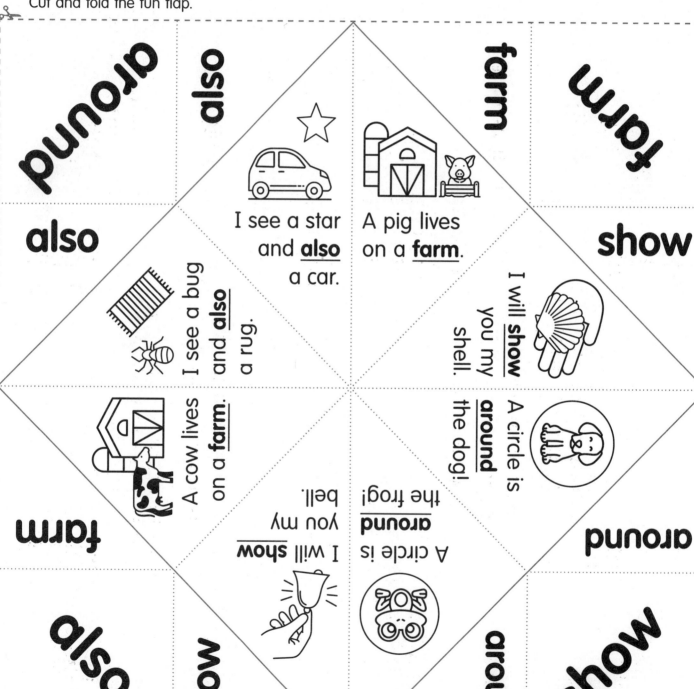

around

also

also

farm

farm

show

I see a star and **also** a car.

A pig lives on a **farm**.

I see a bug and **also** a rug.

I will **show** you my shell.

A cow lives on a **farm**.

A circle is **around** the dog!

I will **show** you my bell.

A circle is **around** the frog!

also

show

show

around

around

show

Name: _____

Trace then practice writing each word.

show show show

also also also also

around around

farm farm farm

FEATURED SIGHT WORDS

three small set put

Cut and fold the fun flap.

set

small

small

put

put

three

It is NOT **small**.

Put the key here.

It is **small**.

There are **three** chairs!

Put the apple here.

This is a tea **set**.

There are **three** bears!

This is a tool **set**.

put

small

three

set

set

three

Name: _____

Trace then practice writing each word.

three three three

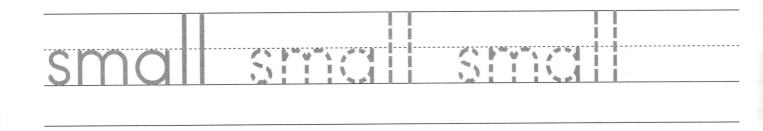

small small small

set set set set set

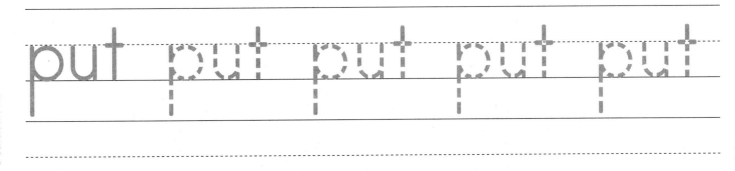

put put put put put

FEATURED SIGHT WORDS

end does another well

Cut and fold the fun flap.

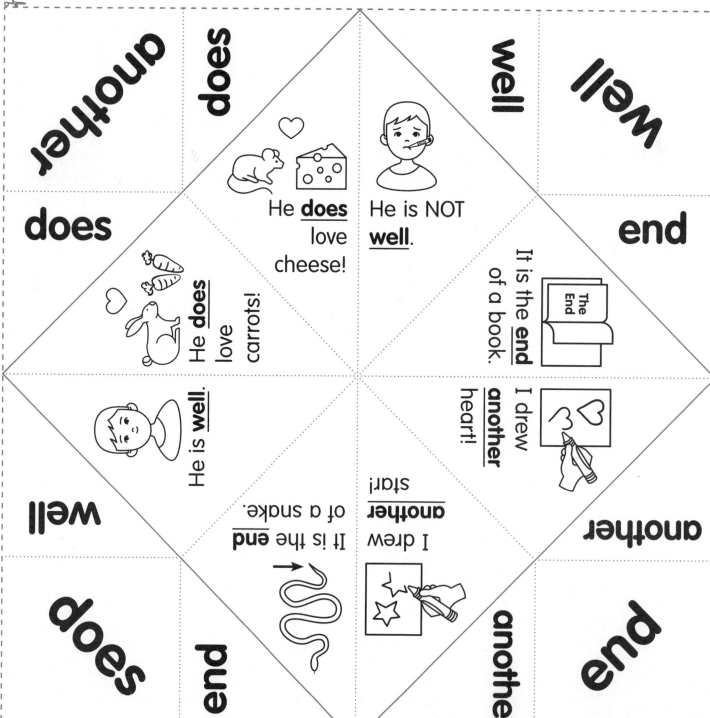

Name: _____

Trace then practice writing each word.

end end end end

does does does

another another

well well well well

FEATURED SIGHT WORDS

large must such even

Cut and fold the fun flap.

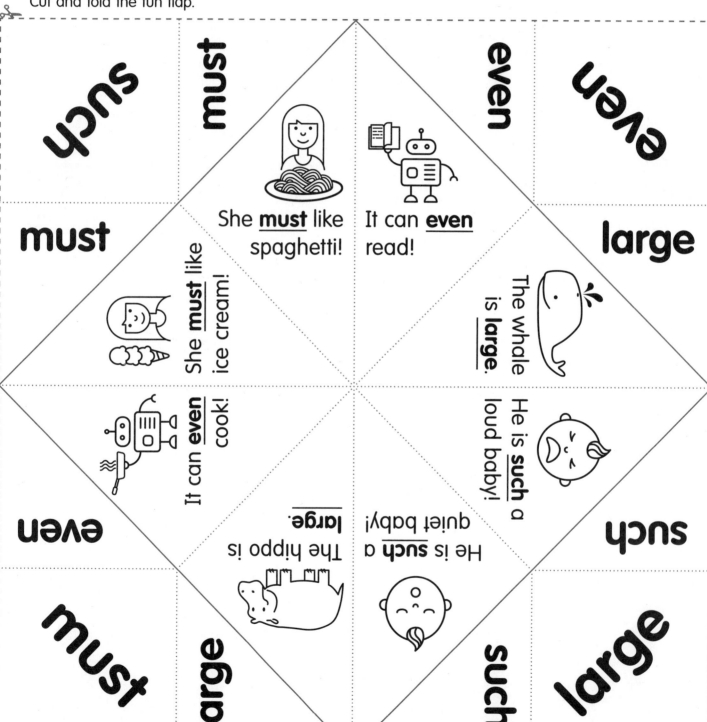

such

must

even

even

must

large

She **must** like spaghetti!

It can **even** read!

She **must** like ice cream!

The whale is **large**.

It can **even** cook!

He is **such** a loud baby!

The hippo is **large**.

He is **such** a quiet baby!

even

such

must

large

such

large

Name: _____

Trace then practice writing each word.

large large large

must must must

such such such

even even even

FEATURED SIGHT WORDS

big because turn here

Cut and fold the fun flap.

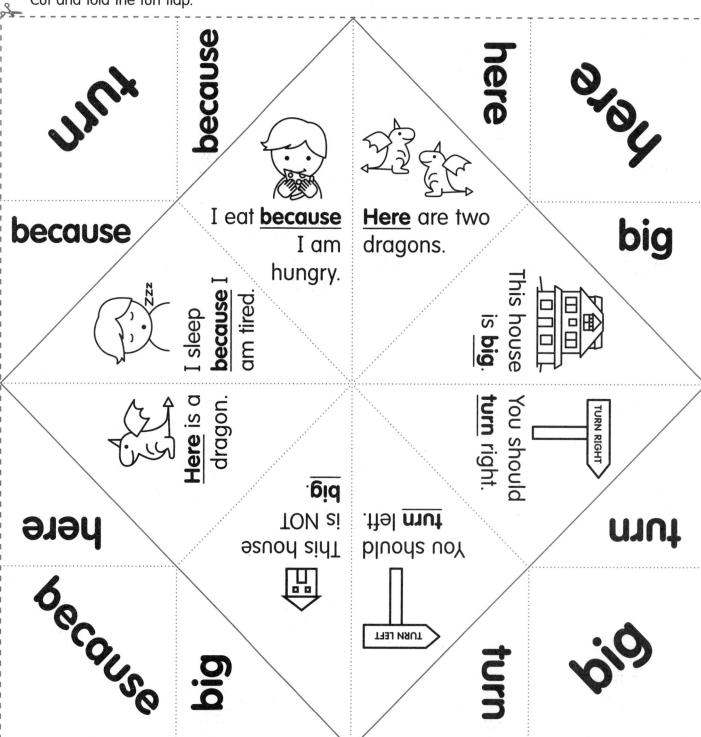

turn

because

because

here

big

I eat **because** I am hungry.

Here are two dragons.

I sleep **because** I am tired.

This house is **big**.

Here is a dragon.

You should **turn** right.

TURN RIGHT

This house is NOT **big**.

You should **turn** left.

TURN LEFT

here

because

big

turn

here

big

turn

big

• © Scholastic Inc.

Name: _____

Trace then practice writing each word.

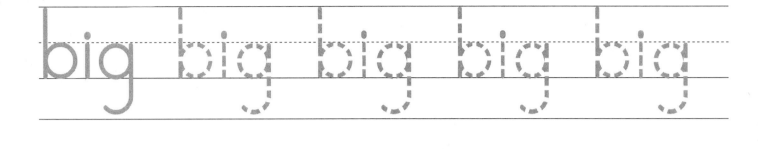

turn turn turn turn

here here here

FEATURED SIGHT WORDS

why asked went men

Cut and fold the fun flap.

went

asked

men

men

asked

why

 I **asked** for scissors.

 Here are three **men**.

I **asked** for crayons.

Why is it snowing?

She **went** on the swing.

Here are two **men**.

Why is it raining?

She **went** on the slide.

men

went

asked

why

went

why

Name: _____

Trace then practice writing each word.

why why why why

asked asked asked

went went went

men men men men

FEATURED SIGHT WORDS

read need land different

Cut and fold the fun flap.

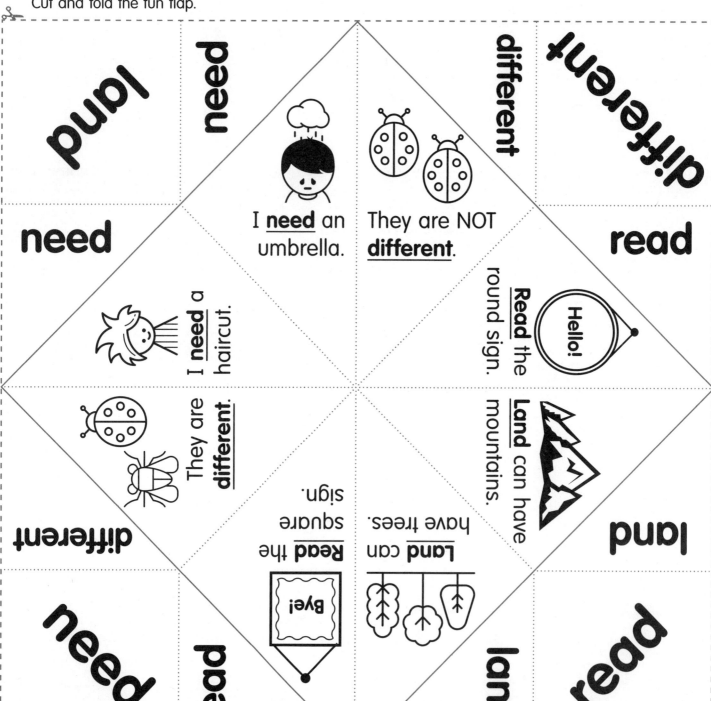

Name: _____

Trace then practice writing each word.

read read read

need need need

land land land

different different

FEATURED SIGHT WORDS

home us move try

Cut and fold the fun flap.

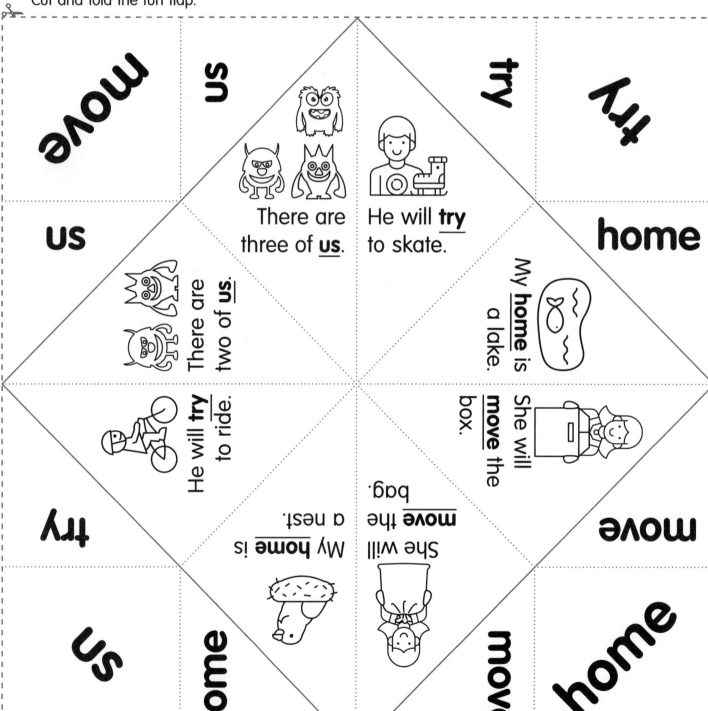

Name: _____

Trace then practice writing each word.

home home home

us us us us us us us

move move move

try try try try try

FEATURED SIGHT WORDS

kind hand picture again

Cut and fold the fun flap.

Name: _____

Trace then practice writing each word.

kind   kind   kind   kind

hand   hand   hand

picture   picture

again   again   again

FEATURED SIGHT WORDS

change off play spell

Cut and fold the fun flap.

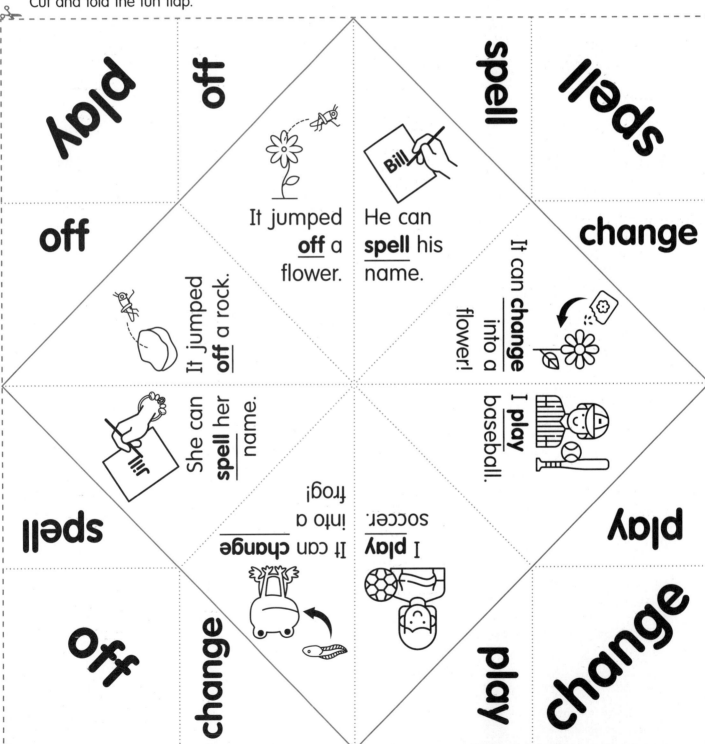

play

off

off

spell

spell

spell

change

It jumped **off** a flower.

He can **spell** his name.

It can **change** into a flower!

It jumped **off** a rock.

I **play** baseball.

She can **spell** her name.

It can **change** into a frog!

I **play** soccer.

off

change

play

play

change

Name: _____

Trace then practice writing each word.

change change

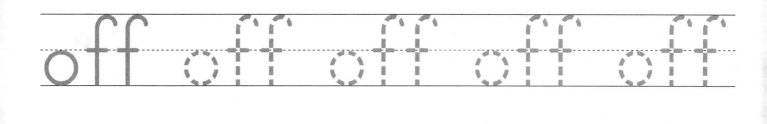

off off off off off

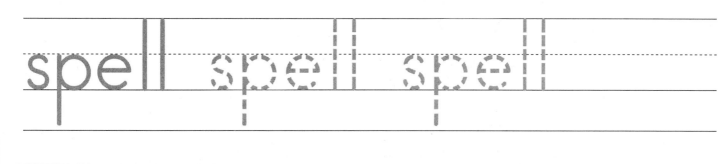

play play play play

spell spell spell

FEATURED SIGHT WORDS

air away animals house

Cut and fold the fun flap.

animals

away

house

house

away

air

The plane flies **away**!

This **house** is made of candy.

The bird flies **away**!

The balloon has **air**.

This **house** is made of bricks.

I see two **animals**.

house

The tire has **air**.

I see three **animals**.

animals

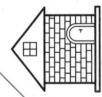

away

air

animals

air

Name: _____

Trace then practice writing each word.

air air air air air

away away away

animals animals

house house house

FEATURED SIGHT WORDS

point page letters mother

Cut and fold the fun flap.

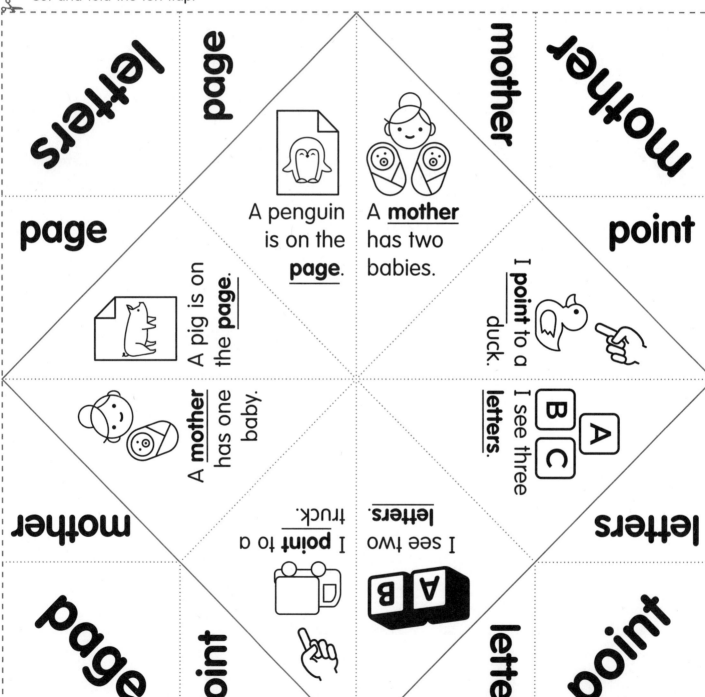

letters

page

mother

page

point

A penguin is on the **page**.

A **mother** has two babies.

I **point** to a duck.

A pig is on the **page**.

A **mother** has one baby.

I see three **letters**.

mother

I **point** to a truck.

I see two **letters**.

letters

page

point

letters

point

Name: _____

Trace then practice writing each word.

point point point

page page page

letters letters

mother mother

FEATURED SIGHT WORDS

answer found study still

Cut and fold the fun flap.

study

found

still

still

found

answer

I **found** a shell!

I **still** have a dollar.

I **found** a feather!

He knows the **answer.**

I **still** have a lollipop.

I do **study.**

still

answer

She knows the **answer.**

I do NOT study.

study

found

answer

study

answer

Name: _____

Trace then practice writing each word.

answer answer

found found found

study study study

still still still still

FEATURED SIGHT WORDS

learn   should   America   world

Cut and fold the fun flap.

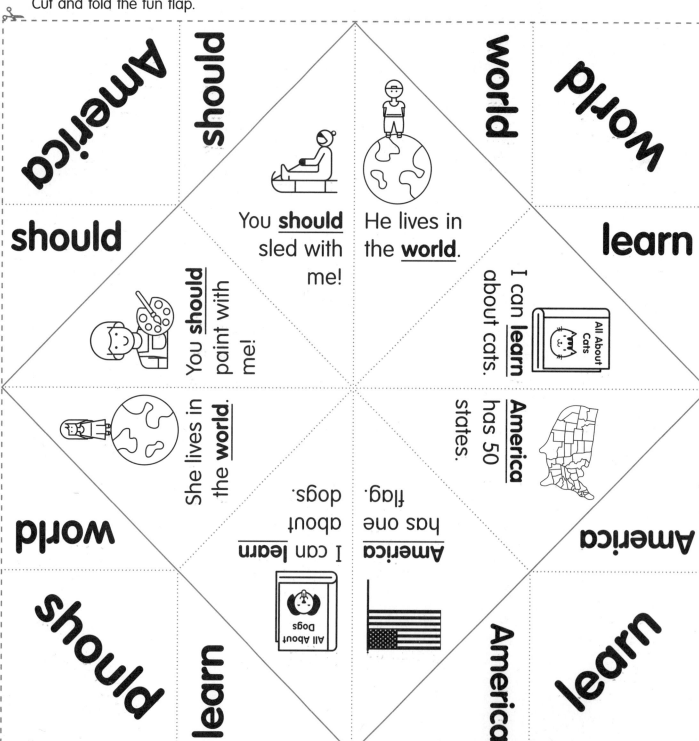

Name: _____

Trace then practice writing each word.

learn learn learn

should should should

America America

world world world

FEATURED SIGHT WORDS

Cut and fold the fun flap.

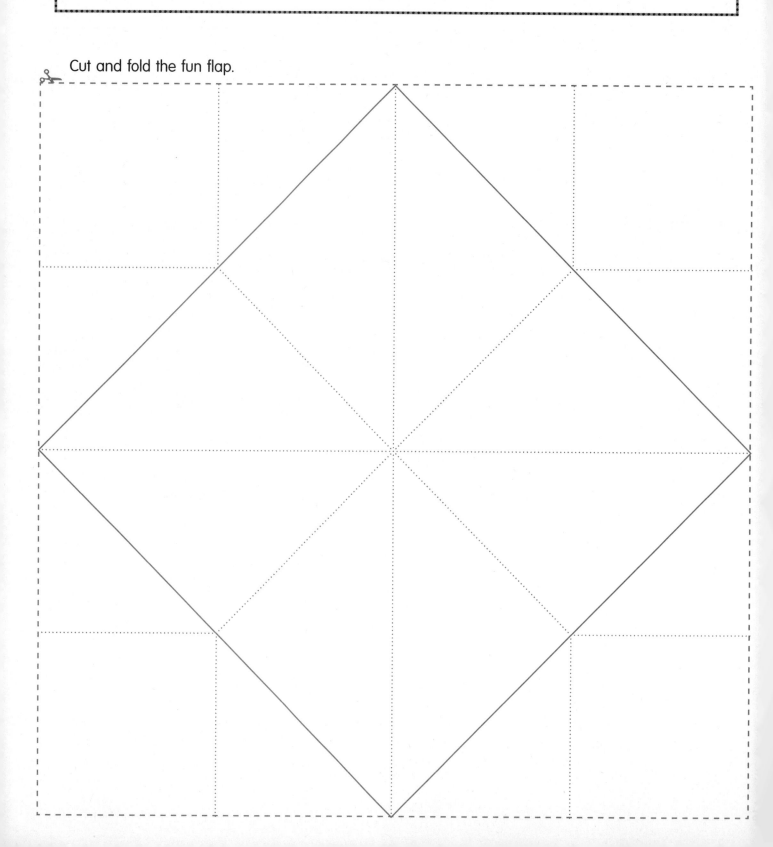

Name: _____

SIGHT WORD ASSESSMENT PART 1

Student's Name: _____

SIGHT WORD	DATE/ ✔ or X	DATE/ ✔ or X	SIGHT WORD	DATE/ ✔ or X	DATE/ ✔ or X
over			say		
new			great		
sound			where		
take			help		
only			through		
little			much		
work			before		
know			line		
place			right		
years			too		
live			means		
me			old		
back			any		
give			same		
most			tell		
very			boy		
after			following		
thing			came		
our			want		
just			show		
name			also		
good			around		
sentence			farm		
man			three		
think			small		

Student's Name: _____

SIGHT WORD	DATE/ ✔ or X	DATE/ ✔ or X	SIGHT WORD	DATE/ ✔ or X	DATE/ ✔ or X
set			try		
put			kind		
end			hand		
does			picture		
another			again		
well			change		
large			off		
must			play		
big			spell		
even			air		
such			away		
because			animals		
turn			house		
here			point		
why			page		
asked			letters		
went			mother		
men			answer		
read			found		
need			study		
land			still		
different			learn		
home			should		
us			America		
move			world		

NOTES